4

Cooking for Dogs

This 2007 edition is published by Gramercy Books, an imprint of Random House Value Publishing, a division of Random House, Inc., New York, by arrangement with New Holland Publishers (UK) Ltd.

Gramercy is a registered trademark and the colophon is a trademark of Random House, Inc.

Random House
New York • Toronto • London • Sydney • Auckland
www.randomhouse.com

Printed and bound in Singapore

A catalog record for this title is available from the Library of Congress.

ISBN: 978-0-517-22983-5

10 9 8 7 6 5 4 3 2 1

Cooking for Dogs

Tempting Recipes for Your Best Friend to Enjoy

Marjorie Walsh

GRAMERCY BOOKS
NEW YORK

Contents

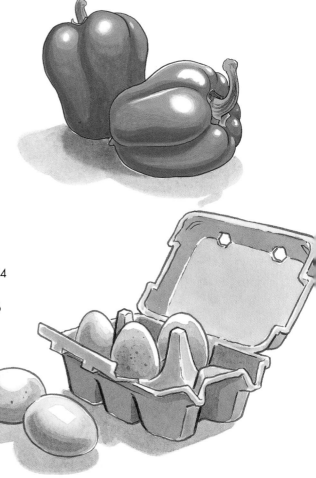

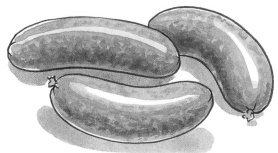

Introduction

When I looked at the nutritional information on commercial pet food and saw by-products, fillers and derivatives I decided that I didn't want to feed that to my dogs. I wouldn't eat these things, so why should our dogs? I started out by just making extra food when cooking the family's meals, so that our dogs ate what we ate. Because I wanted to get it right, I did a lot of research and invested in some nutritional software. The end result is happy, healthy dogs with coats like velvet, plenty of energy, and hardly any pooping.

There is no mystery or magic to feeding your pet well. A review of just a few of the books that are available on feeding your pet and the nutritional information on commercial dog food labels shows that the experts don't really know what makes the perfect dog food. Breeders and vets will have their favorite foods, too. So, how do you know?

Dogs are like humans: all different. Some can eat anything and everything. Some have sensitive tummies and some specific breeds have specific problems. For example, deep-chested dogs like Newfoundlands can be prone to twisted gut, a serious condition. For larger dogs it is much kinder to put their feed bowl in a stand adjusted for their height so that they are not stooping to eat their food. A side bonus is that their bowl stays in one place and they don't have to push it round the floor to get that last morsel. It is

a matter of trial and error to find foods that eliminate any possible health problems. Try different foods and different food combinations until you find one to suit.

For all dogs, just be guided by your pet. If he or she is happy, with a glossy coat, bright eyes, active, and with regular, firm stools, then you're feeding the right food. And if you can feel the ribs, you are feeding the right quantity.

The only golden rule is to add calcium to every meal; approximately ⅛–¼ teaspoon should be sufficient. In most foodstuffs the phosphorous to calcium ratio is inverse to needs, which means that the phosphorous element usually exceeds the calcium level. If we don't adjust this imbalance, not only are we not getting enough calcium, but over time, the excess phosphorous will leech calcium from dogs' bones, making them brittle and prone to breaks.

How do you get calcium? Two ways. First, if you like eggs, simply save the eggshells, wash and bake in an oven at 180°C/350°F, for about 30 minutes. Then reduce to a powder form either in a food processor or with a mortar and pestle. If you want it really fine, put it through a coffee grinder after the food processor. Otherwise you can just buy calcium tablets from a health food store and crush them finely.

All of the recipes in this book are made with foods that humans eat. In theory then, you can make any of these meals for your own dinner and then take a portion for your pet, add calcium, and with one cooking session everyone in the family is fed. You will also see that some of the recipes contain a small amount of liver. This to ensure that your doggie gets his or her B12 requirement.

Please check the nutritional information. Some of the recipes can be used for regular feeding but others should only be offered occasionally. We think of dogs as meat eaters, but actually they are omnivores and don't need as much protein as is commonly believed. As a guide, their meal should consist of 25% protein, 30% fat and 45% carbohydrates.

This nutritional information is based on the needs of an average 22kg (50lb) dog, that is a house pet with regular outdoor activity. If your pet is smaller just reduce the portion size accordingly. For example, for a dog of 11kg (25lb), either halve the recipe size when cooking or simply halve the portion size given. For a larger dog, increase similarly. For a working dog or lactating bitch, double the portion size. For older or infirm dogs, give them portion sizes that keep them happy.

Serving sizes are based on two meals a day; breakfast and an evening meal, with a little room left for a small snack. If you don't have time for breakfast in your house, just increase the serving size for the one meal.

So, armed with this information you can actually share your evening meal with your pet, remembering to add calcium to their portion. Dogs also need fat for energy so their meat should not be too lean, and don't get too hung up on calories. Just be guided by your pet. And, as we all know, just because a dog keeps looking for food does not mean that you are not offering enough food. Like some humans, some dogs are just food-focused and always on the lookout for something to eat.

How easy is it? Well just cook extra, either from one of these recipes or from your own evening meal. Divide into portions and either refrigerate or freeze the excess for later use so you have ready-made meals on hand when you have run out of dog food.

Go on, give your pooch a change from canned or dried food!

MARJORIE WALSH

Nutrition primer

A dog's life then and now: a brief history of feeding

When dogs were wild, they devoted much of their daily activity to hunting. For about 3,000 years after domestication, dogs ate whatever food was left for them at the end of a meal. It was a scrappy, tough existence. In 1922, a group of American businessmen started a new industry, deciding that horsemeat unsuitable for human consumption could be converted into dog food. Gradually, complex formulas and elaborate ingredients for dog food came into vogue. Generally speaking, modern dog food is well balanced.

Although today's dog no longer must search out food, mealtime remains a central aspect of his/her life. From the person in charge of feeding to the diet itself, routine is one of the most important factors affecting a dog's behavior. Routine helps to ensure a good appetite, digestion, and regular eliminations.

Did you know?

A diet consisting of 100% meat is entirely inadequate. Meat contains no calcium, so a diet of all meat will cause a deficiency of this mineral which is essential for bone and muscle health. Low- or no-fat meat is missing the dog's best source of energy. This causes protein to be used as an energy source, which means the dog feels hungry all the time. To aid digestion, all types of carbohydrates need to be boiled, baked or toasted before feeding to a dog. Starches from oats, corn, and potatoes in particular are difficult to digest unless cooked. On the other hand, white and whole-wheat bread are two of the best natural foods to include. Actually, minerals are most critical for canine health, especially calcium and phosphorus. Dogs often require some supplement of these in part because commercial food ingredients (meat, meat by-products, soybeans, casein, and eggs) contain low levels of both, and in the wrong ratio. Milk and bone meal are excellent sources to supply calcium and phosphorus, as well as magnesium, in easily digested form.

Energy

A dog needs energy more than anything. And for that, s/he needs calories. Lots of them. This is one of the most important, fundamental requirements. It relates directly to how much food the dog must consume every day. This is critical for a dog owner to keep in mind. Most people think of calories as something to be avoided as much as possible. But a calorie is a measurement of energy potential. That means, in simplified terms, that the more calories in your dog's food, the greater energy potential it contains (more on this later). If the food is high in calories – 'high caloric density' – then your dog doesn't need as much food to supply his or her daily need for fuel (energy).

Table scraps

Dogs existed for thousands of years eating table scraps. It's logical to think that table scraps would be an ideal way to improve the overall nutritive value of a dog's diet. However, just as dog food has changed over the years, so too has the food at our tables. With the advent of commercial dog food, fewer dogs eat table scraps. And as human food has become more commercially prepared, its suitability as dog food has declined. Table scraps have plenty of calories, but with little else that is usable by the dog's body systems. Table scraps can improve the palatability of commercial food, but they must be finely chopped and blended together.

- **Fact:** Most table scraps are composed of fats and carbohydrates, with lots of calories, but contain little else in the way of nutritional value.
- **Fact:** Dogs often prefer the taste of table scraps to more balanced commercial food. If not mixed well together, the dog may eat only the table scraps and leave the rest.

Choosing the right food

The most reliable way to judge the nutritional value of a dog's food is to see what happens when s/he eats. Is s/he always hungry? Coat dull or glossy? Active or lethargic? Of course, these are just a few signs which can also signal other problems. But for starters, you can eliminate:

- unripe tomatoes and the green tomato plant – can cause irritation to the stomach
- chocolate – contains theobromine which is poisonous to dogs
- chicken bones – these can splinter and irritate the gut
- onions – contain chemicals which can be poisonous to dogs
- macadamia nuts – have been known to cause temporary paralysis in dogs
- dried fruit
- uncooked eggs – the raw egg white contains biotin which cannot be absorbed
- canned food containing more than 78% water
- any food whose guaranteed calcium content is less than 0.30%
- any food without at least one cereal grain

Digestibility

Digestibility is the reason for all this information about types of food and ratios. A food may contain the exact balance required, but if the ingredients used for that food are indigestible, the dog will starve. When a dog's food is made well, from ingredients approaching full digestibility, s/he may produce a stool only two to three times a week. When the digestive system can break down a food completely, and absorb its nutritive content, there is little waste.

In general, animal food sources are more digestible than plants. However, most carbohydrates come from plants. And cellulose, which makes up a large portion of plant carbohydrate, cannot be digested. Dogs' digestive systems do not contain the right enzymes for the job. Thus alfalfa, which contains virtually every nutrient a dog needs, is useless because the dog cannot digest it. Yet gelatin is equally unsuitable because, while it is highly digestible, it lacks two essential amino acids.

Teasing the palate

The commercial food industry tends to overlook food palatability from a dog's standpoint. Flavors and odors are more likely to be negative factors in a dog's interest in food. Dogs also care about the texture of their food, and some studies have shown that a low-salt diet is preferred almost two to one. Freshly made food is often sold frozen, but this should not be considered a negative selling point. On the contrary, frozen food will retain its fresh flavor longer and tends to be rated highest by discerning dogs. Frozen food is highly digestible, tasty, and desirable to the dog. Frozen food should be served at room temperature.

> Recommended daily allowances: Calories 1350kcal; Protein 48g; Carbohydrates 186g; Fiber 18.9g; Fat 42g; Calcium 2700 mg

Breakfasts

This section contains recipes for healthy breakfasts and occasional treats, some for the calorie conscious and some for those with intolerances. Egg is almost the perfect dog food, so dish up these recipes knowing that you are giving your pet something good.

Slimline cereal

Preparation time: 5 minutes • Cooking time: 0 minutes • Servings: 1

A slimline breakfast that gives bulk with few calories.

Ingredients

1 Weetabix or 5 Tbsp equivalent cereal

⅛ tsp calcium

240ml/8fl oz/1 cup skimmed milk

120ml/4fl oz/½ cup water

Method

• Place the Weetabix or equivalent cereal in the dog bowl.
Add the calcium. Pour over the milk and water mixture. Serve.

Note: slightly warm the milk or use warm water so that the breakfast
is just like comfort food; warm and moist.

Nutritional info per serving: Calories 153kcal; Protein 10g;
Carbohydrates 26g; Fiber 2g; Fat 0.95g; Calcium 682mg

Light scrambled egg

Preparation time: 5 minutes • Cooking time: 5 minutes • Servings: 1

You can add cereal and replace the skimmed milk with

full fat milk to increase the calories in this breakfast by a third

to the full breakfast version.

Ingredients

2 eggs

140ml/5fl oz/⅔ cup skimmed milk

⅛ tsp calcium

Method

● Break the eggs into a non-stick pan over medium heat, add the milk and stir until cooked. Pour into a dog bowl, add the calcium and mix in. Let cool to room temperature and serve.

Nutritional info per serving: Calories 256kcal; Protein 19g; Carbohydrates 10g; Fiber 0g; Fat 15½g; Calcium 615mg

Smoked haddock and eggs

Preparation time: 5 minutes • Cooking time: 5 minutes • Servings: 1

A breakfast for pooches who are lactose intolerant, on dry food, and who need a high number of calories. If your pet doesn't need this many calories, this quantity can make two servings. Also perfect if you don't want to feed your pet red meat. Dogs love fish: the smellier, the better!

Ingredients

55g/2oz smoked haddock, flaked

1 tsp sunflower oil

3 eggs

1 English muffin, toasted

¼ tsp calcium

Method

- Poach the haddock in water or milk for 5–10 minutes. Heat oil in non-stick pan. Break eggs into pan, add flakes of fish and stir until cooked.

- Toast muffin. Put egg and fish mixture into dog bowl. Tear muffin into bite sized pieces, add to egg and fish. Add calcium and mix well. Serve.

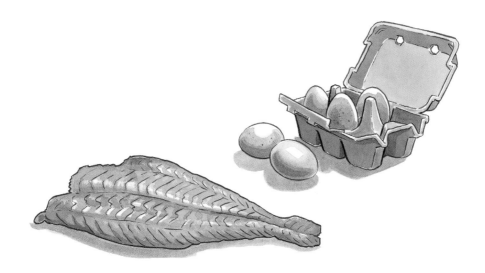

Nutritional info per serving: Calories 675kcal; Protein 45g;
Carbohydrates 57g; Fiber 9g; Fat 30g; Calcium 1181mg

Eggs and sausage

Preparation time: 5 minutes • Cooking time: 12 minutes • Servings: 1

A breakfast you can share with your pet, this is a meat recipe

for a lactose intolerant pet. If your pet is not lactose intolerant, you can

add a little milk (about 80ml/2¾fl oz/⅓ cup) to make it more moist.

Talk about chop lickin'!

Ingredients

1 sausage (about 2oz/55g)

1 tsp sunflower or corn oil

2 eggs

1 slice whole wheat bread, toasted

¼ tsp calcium

Method

- Grill sausage, cut into bite-sized pieces, and leave to cool.

- Heat oil in non-stick pan. Break eggs into pan (add milk, if using) and stir until cooked. Stir in cooked sausage.

- Place egg and sausage mixture into dog bowl and while it is cooling, toast bread. Tear into bite-sized pieces and stir into the egg and sausage together with the calcium. Serve at room temperature.

Nutritional info per serving: Calories 460kcal; Protein 27g; Carbohydrates 15g; Fiber 2g; Fat 32g; Calcium 800mg

Bacon, avocado, and cheese omelette

Preparation time: 10 minutes • Cooking time: 6 minutes • Servings: 2

A very special breakfast that you can either share with your pet or serve as a birthday treat. This is a substantial breakfast in terms of calories so if you and your pet are weight-watching, serve half (or halve the ingredients to make 1 small omelette). Avocado is great for a shiny coat.

Ingredients

75g/2½oz fresh tomatoes, chopped

2 Tbsp fresh coriander, chopped
or 1 tsp dried coriander

1 Tbsp fresh lime juice

3 strips bacon

1 small avocado

4 eggs

2 Tbsp water

1 Tbsp sunflower or corn oil

50g/2oz/½ cup cheddar cheese,
grated

½ tsp calcium

Method

- In a small bowl mix chopped tomatoes, coriander, and lime juice to make a dog-friendly salsa. Grill bacon and leave to cool. Peel the avocado. Remove the stone and cut the flesh into 1cm (½in) pieces. Cut the bacon into bite-sized pieces.

- In a bowl, whisk the eggs and water. In either an omelette pan or non-stick frying pan, heat the oil. Pour the egg mixture to cover the bottom of the pan. Cook until almost set. Over half the egg mixture, put the bacon, avocado and cheese. Fold the other half of the egg over the top and cook until set.

- Allow to cool to room temperature and serve together with the salsa. Cut the omelette into pieces if your pet is small.

Nutritional info per serving: Calories 650kcal; Protein 26g; Carbohydrates 13g; Fiber 7.5g; Fat 56g; Calcium 1000mg

Speedy Meals
and Fast Food

We all know that there is not always time to cook fancy evening meals. All of the recipes in this section can be ready in 30 minutes or less. And in some cases, you can reduce the time even further by using canned or frozen vegetables, pre-cooking rice, and using leftover cooked meat. And there are a couple of vegetable dishes that you can use with any meal which is predominately protein, from any of the other chapters.

Honeyed chicken

Preparation time: 10 minutes • Cooking time: 5 minutes • Servings: 1

This recipe has been designed to make use of cooked chicken but you can use fresh chicken (see method for details). Add a portion of the Stir-fried bean salad (see page 32) to make the perfect meal. The nutritional information is based on the chicken dish with the Stir-fried bean salad on the side.

Ingredients

1 Tbsp olive oil	120g/4oz cooked chicken, diced
2 garlic cloves, crushed	6 anchovies
3 Tbsp honey	¼ tsp calcium
Grated lemon rind	240ml/8fl oz/1 cup chicken stock
1 tsp dried rosemary	Stir-fried bean salad (see page 32)

Method

• Heat oil in pan, sauté garlic for 1 minute. Add honey, lemon rind and rosemary and stir until the honey is liquid. Remove from heat. Stir in chicken, anchovies and calcium. Add chicken stock and mix well.

• Place in dog bowl, add portion of Stir-fried bean salad, and serve at room temperature.

Note: if you want to use fresh chicken, cut into bite-sized pieces and sauté in a pan with garlic until cooked through (about 5 minutes). Then follow recipe as for cooked chicken.

Nutritional info per serving: Calories 1298kcal; Protein 84g; Carbohydrates 141g; Fiber 21g; Fat 45g; Calcium 1745mg

Lamb with spinach

Preparation time: 10 minutes • Cooking time: 6 minutes • Servings: 1

If your pooch has adventurous tastes, this lamb with a

Japanese twist will be a treat.

Ingredients

1 Tbsp sesame oil

2 garlic cloves, crushed

1 apple, cored and cut into
bite-sized pieces

¼ tsp ground mixed spice

280g/10oz spinach

3 Tbsp rice wine, white wine
vinegar, or cider vinegar

1 tsp cornflour, dissolved in
1 Tbsp water

250g/8oz cooked lamb,
cut into bite-sized pieces

½ tsp calcium

540g/20oz/3 cups pasta or rice

Method

• Heat oil in wok or frying pan. Add garlic and stir-fry for 1 minute.
Add apple and stir-fry for a further minute. Stir in ground mixed spice.
Add spinach and stir-fry for 1 minute or until just wilted. Add rice wine and the
cornflour mixture to wok. Stir-fry for 1 minute. Remove from heat, add lamb and
calcium and stir until well mixed.

• At the same time, bring a pan of water to a boil and cook pasta or rice
according to the instructions. Drain and run under cold water.

• Put pasta or rice into the dog bowl, add lamb mixture and mix well.
Serve at room temperature.

Note: if you want to use fresh lamb, stir-fry it with the garlic for 2–3 minutes.

Nutritional info per serving: Calories 1412kcal; Protein 84g;
Carbohydrates 143g; Fiber 20g; Fat 55g; Calcium 1800mg

Stir-fried bean salad

Preparation time: 10 minutes • Cooking time: 8 minutes • Servings: 3

A vegetable and bean dish that can be divided into three servings and
eaten as a whole meal, or smaller servings used as a side dish.

Ingredients

170g/6oz green beans,
cut into 3cm (2in) pieces

170g/6oz runner beans,
cut into 3cm (2in) pieces

140g/5oz snow peas

2 Tbsp olive oil

2 cloves garlic, crushed

450g/16oz canned red kidney
beans, drained and mashed

425g/15oz canned cannellini
beans, drained and mashed

340g/12oz canned
sweet corn, drained

225g/8oz cheddar
cheese, cubed

3 Tbsp fresh parsley, chopped

¾ tsp calcium

Method

- Half-fill a saucepan with water. Bring to a boil, then add green and runner beans and simmer for 2 minutes. Add snow peas, bring back to a boil, and then drain and rinse under cold water.

- Heat oil in a wok or frying pan. Add garlic and stir-fry 1–2 minutes. Stir in kidney beans, cannellini beans and sweet corn. Stir-fry for 3 minutes. Remove from heat. Add cheese, parsley, and calcium and toss everything together to mix.

- If serving as main meal, put one-third into dog bowl and serve at room temperature. Put the remainder in a bowl, cover and refrigerate. Use within 3 days.

Note: you can use any vegetables that you have on hand: fresh, canned, frozen. If you do not have fresh parsley either omit or use 1 tsp dried parsley.

Nutritional info per serving: Calories 1120kcal; Protein 63g; Carbohydrates 131g; Fiber 34g; Fat 38g; Calcium 1544mg

Greek-style vegetables

Preparation time: 10 minutes • Cooking time: 4 minutes • Servings: 1

A low protein dish that can be a meal on its own or divided into

3 servings and added to other meals.

Ingredients

2 Tbsp oil

½ tsp dried oregano

1 clove garlic, crushed

1 Tbsp balsamic vinegar

340g/12oz red or yellow
cherry tomatoes

50g/1½oz/½ cup feta cheese,
crumbled

675g/1½lb broad beans, frozen or
fresh (shelled)

½ tsp calcium

Method

- Heat oil in wok or frying pan. Add garlic, tomatoes, broad beans, and oregano. Stir-fry 3–4 minutes over medium heat until beans are tender. Stir in balsamic vinegar. Stir-fry for a further minute.

- Remove from heat, add cheese and calcium and toss to mix. Serve at room temperature in a dog bowl.

Nutritional info per serving: Calories 1265kcal; Protein 65g; Carbohydrates 154g; Fiber 41g; Fat 47g; Calcium 2108mg

Paw lickin' pizza

Preparation time: 10 minutes • Cooking time: 20 minutes • Servings: 2

Don't wait for pizza delivery; whip this one up for your loved one! The recipe has been divided into two servings but if your pooch can't resist and needs some special treatment, let him/her eat the whole pizza!

Ingredients

70ml/2½fl oz/⅓ cup tomato purée

70ml/2½fl oz/⅓ cup water

1 Tbsp corn oil

¼ tsp garlic powder

½ tsp calcium

1 store-bought pizza crust

50g/1½oz mixed vegetables, cubed

110g/4oz cooked beef, cut into small cubes

25g/¾oz/¼ cup cheddar cheese, grated

Method

• Preheat oven to 200°C/400°F. Mix the first five ingredients together and spread over the pizza crust. Place vegetables and beef on top and sprinkle the cheese over everything. Bake for 20–25 minutes or until top is golden. Leave to cool, then slice.

Note: you can make your own pizza crust if you wish, but using a store-bought pizza crust means that this dinner can be whipped up in next to no time.

Nutritional info per serving: Calories 905kcal; Protein 42g; Carbohydrates 125g; Fiber 7g; Fat 25g; Calcium 900mg

Chompin' chicken nuggets

Preparation time: 10 minutes • Cooking time: 20 minutes • Servings: 2

Yummy, yummy, yummy. A special treat only, because while this is low in

protein, it's quite high in fat. You can add your own vegetables or use

one of the vegetable recipes from this book as a side dish.

Ingredients

2 chicken breasts

140g/5oz/1 cup
whole wheat flour

1 tsp garlic powder

½ tsp calcium

1 egg

250ml/8⅓fl oz/1¼ cups milk

8 Weetabix (or equivalent cereal)

120ml/4fl oz/½ cup corn oil

Method

• Cut the chicken breasts into small cubes. Mix together the flour, garlic powder, and calcium. Whisk the egg and milk together and add to the flour mix to make a batter. Crush the cereal.

• Drop the chicken cubes into the batter, then roll in the cereal.

• Shallow fry in the oil for about 20 minutes.
(They can also be deep-fried.) Serve cool.

Nutritional info per serving: Calories 1240kcal; Protein 53g;
Carbohydrates 108g; Fiber 16g; Fat 68g; Calcium 1411mg

Hound dog hamburger

Preparation time: 10 minutes • Cooking time: 20 minutes • Servings: 1

A healthy hamburger which looks pretty spectacular and which your

doggie will love – he/she won't wait to appreciate the look of it!

Ingredients

3 large sweet potatoes

225g/8oz minced beef

½ tsp rosemary, dried

½ tsp calcium

2 Weetabix, crushed or
8 Tbsp equivalent cereal

½ tsp cod liver oil

60g/2oz frozen peas or sweet corn
or mixture of both

Method

- Peel and cut potatoes. Boil until tender and then mash. Leave to cool.

- While potatoes are cooking, mix remaining ingredients together in a bowl. Form into one large pattie. Grill until cooked through, approximately 20 minutes.

- Divide cold mashed potatoes in half. Shape each half into a large patty. Place one potato patty on the bottom, add the hamburger and top with the second potato patty. Serve at room temperature.

Note: if you don't have any cod liver oil in the cupboard, substitute sunflower or corn oil.

Nutritional info per serving: Calories 960kcal; Protein 75g; Carbohydrates 122g; Fiber 19g; Fat 18g; Calcium 1638mg

Fish 'n' chips

Preparation time: 5 minutes • Cooking time: 10 minutes • Servings: 1

A perfect midday snack or a light evening meal.

Ingredients

2 eggs

280g/10oz/2 cups flour

2 pieces of cod (or other white fish)

120ml/4fl oz/½ cup oil

1 medium portion frozen french fries

Method

• Beat the eggs and pour into a bowl. Put the flour into another bowl.
Coat the cod with the egg and then dip into the flour, coating both sides.

• Heat the oil in a frying pan and fry the cod until cooked through, about
3–4 minutes each side. Cook the french fries according to instructions on package.
Let cool. Break the cod into bite-sized pieces and place in bowl with fries.
Serve at room temperature.

Note: you could replace the frozen french fries with any fried cooked potatoes – a
good use for leftover potatoes.

Nutritional info per serving: Calories 506kcal; Protein 12g;
Carbohydrates 60g; Fiber 5g; Fat 25g; Calcium 30mg

Poochie's potatoes

Preparation time: 15 minutes • Cooking time: 15 minutes • Servings: 2

A side dish for Chompin' chicken nuggets (see page 38)

or for adding to any other meat dish.

Ingredients

500g/17oz cooked potatoes, diced

1 Tbsp mixed vegetables, frozen, canned, or fresh

50g/2oz/½ cup cottage cheese

1 Tbsp brewer's yeast

2 Tbsp diced carrots, cooked

⅛ tsp calcium

60ml/2fl oz/¼ cup milk

1½ tsp corn oil

50g/1¾oz/½ cup cheddar cheese, grated

Method

- Preheat the oven to 170°C/350°F. Layer the first six ingredients in a casserole dish. Pour the milk and oil over. Sprinkle with the grated cheese.

- Bake for about 15 minutes at 170°C/350°F until the cheese melts and the top is slightly brown. Cool before serving.

Note: You can substitute the potatoes with 500g/17oz/3 cups cooked oatmeal or cooked brown rice

Nutritional info per serving: Calories 497kcal; Protein 21g;
Carbohydrates 53g; Fiber 5g; Fat 23g; Calcium 478mg

Special Occasions and Exotic Meals

All the major holidays are represented here, although for pooch's own birthday you will need to go to the Snacks and Treats section for a delicious cake. All of these recipes can be made with fresh ingredients or you can use up food left over from your own holiday celebrations. There is also a selection of delicious Mediterranean dishes when you want an exotic, but healthy, meal.

Valentine love apple cake

Preparation time: 10 minutes • Cooking time: 1¼ hours • Servings: 10

What is a love apple? The French originally called tomatoes *pomme d'amour*, or love apples, so this gorgeous dessert is a great addition to a pooch's Valentine party. Each serving should be about 75g/2½oz.

Ingredients

1 can condensed tomato soup

1 tsp baking soda

2 eggs

½ tsp calcium

35g/1¼oz/¼ cup brown sugar

280g/10oz/2 cups
whole wheat flour

1 tsp ground cinnamon

½ Tbsp ground cloves

1 small bottle or can of
maraschino cherries

strawberry, raspberry or black cherry
preserves (optional)

Method

- Preheat oven to 160°C/325°F. In a mixing bowl, stir baking soda into the soup. Lightly beat eggs and add to the soup mix. Then combine the rest of the ingredients, except preserves, and mix thoroughly.

- Pour into a 15-cm (6-in) heart-shaped cake pan or a 23 x 13 x 8-cm (9 x 5 x 3-in) loaf pan. Bake for 55 minutes–1¼ hours or until a toothpick comes out clean when inserted in the center of the cake.

- Cool for 5 minutes in the pan, then remove and place on wire rack to cool completely. If you want to make it really special for Valentine's Day, spread a little strawberry, raspberry or black cherry preserves on the top before serving a slice in a dog bowl.

Nutritional info per serving: Calories 178kcal; Protein 5g; Carbohydrates 26g; Fiber 4g; Fat 7g; Calcium 169mg

Pumpkin cauldron

Preparation time: 20 minutes • Cooking time: 55 minutes • Servings: 1

A yummy Halloween treat, especially for young dogs. How much food you will get depends on the size of the pumpkin. The nutritional analysis is based on 5–6 cups of cooked mixture, which will be equal to one serving.

Ingredients

1 pumpkin	3½oz Tbsp flour
2 chicken breasts	570ml/1 pint/2½ cups chicken stock
2 Tbsp olive oil	1 cinnamon stick
2 red peppers	1 bay leaf
55g/2oz bacon	2 Tbsp fresh parsley, chopped
1 clove garlic, crushed	½ tsp calcium

Method

- Pre-heat oven to 190°C/375°F. Cut the top off the pumpkin to make a lid. Scoop out the seeds. Cut the flesh from the insides, being careful not to cut the skin. Cut flesh into bite-sized pieces.

- Cut the chicken into bite-sized pieces. Heat the oil in a frying pan and fry chicken until golden but not cooked through. Remove. De-seed the peppers and cut into bite-sized pieces. Cut the bacon into bite-sized pieces. Add the garlic, peppers and bacon to the pan. Cook for 2–3 minutes. Stir in the flour and cook for 1 minute. Add the stock and bring to a boil. Add the chicken, pumpkin, cinnamon stick, and bay leaf.

- Pour the mixture into the pumpkin, put lid on and bake for about 45 minutes or until the chicken is cooked through. Stir in the parsley and calcium. Spoon some into the dog bowl (without the cinnamon stick and bayleaf!) and serve at room temperature.

Nutritional info per serving: Calories 1316kcal; Protein 86g; Carbohydrates 102g; Fiber 20g; Fat 67g; Calcium 1676mg

Turkey cranberry stew

Preparation time: 10 minutes • Cooking time: 6 minutes • Servings: 1

A yummy way to use up that leftover turkey at Christmas to give your pet

a dog-licious dinner.

Ingredients

225g/8oz sweet potatoes

225g/8oz squash or pumpkin

110g/4oz celery

250g/8½oz cooked turkey, diced

240g/8⅓fl oz/1 cup turkey stock

2 Tbsp flour

55g/2oz cranberries,
fresh or dried

½ tsp calcium

Method

- Peel and dice potatoes and squash, cut celery into bite-sized pieces. Boil in a saucepan for 3–4 minutes, until just starting to soften. Add cooked turkey to the saucepan.

- Whisk the flour into the cold turkey stock. Add turkey stock to the pan and simmer for 10 minutes, stirring occasionally. Add cranberries and mix well. Remove from heat and place in dog bowl. Stir in calcium and serve at room temperature.

Nutritional info per serving: Calories 1090kcal; Protein 88g; Carbohydrates 120g; Fiber 18g; Fat 30g; Calcium 1717mg

Dog nog

Preparation time: 10 minutes • Cooking time: 40 minutes • Servings: 8

A special Christmas treat for your pet.

Ingredients

1 chicken breast

1.4 L/2½ pints/6 cups water

140g/5oz/1 cup whole wheat flour

2 eggs, beaten

⅛ tsp parsley, dried

Method

- Boil chicken breast for about ½ hour and remove from water to cool. Add flour to chicken water and beat out any lumps. Add beaten eggs. Cook on low heat until mixture has thickened. Mince chicken in food processor and add to the gravy. Add a little more water if needed to get a pourable liquid.

- Place in dog bowl, sprinkle with parsley and serve at room temperature.

Note: To reduce preparation and cooking time, use leftover cooked chicken.

Nutritional info per serving: Calories 90kcal; Protein 7g;
Carbohydrates 11g; Fiber 2g; Fat 2g; Calcium 18mg

Roasted root vegetables

Preparation time: 15 minutes • Cooking time: 30 minutes • Servings: 2

The recipes that follow in this section do not have any green vegetables,

so this dish is the perfect addition to any of them. Alternatively, add

285g/10oz cooked turkey, diced, and 2 tsp calcium to make it a

complete meal of its own.

Ingredients

950ml/1⅔ pints/4 cups fruit juice (apple or cranberry)

225g/8oz carrots

225g/8oz sweet potatoes

225g/8oz turnips

225g/8oz rutabaga

225g/8oz parsnips

3 Tbsp butter

Method

- Boil juice until it is reduced to 1 cup, about 30 minutes.
Pre-heat oven to 220°C/425°F.

- Peel and dice root vegetables and place in roasting pan. Whisk the butter into the reduced juice and pour over vegetables. Toss to coat. Roast until vegetables are golden and tender, stirring occasionally, about 30 minutes.

- Allow to cool to room temperature and serve with a main dish.

Nutritional info per serving: Calories 486kcal; Protein 6g;
Carbohydrates 80g; Fiber 18g; Fat 18g; Calcium 2270mg

Mediterranean prawn casserole

Preparation time: 10 minutes • Cooking time: 35 minutes • Servings: 1

We know that Mediterranean dishes are healthy. Watch this get woofed

down and know that you are giving your loved one super-goodness!

Ingredients

250g/8½oz whole wheat pasta

3 garlic cloves, crushed

560g/1¼lb canned plum
tomatoes, chopped

70ml/2½fl oz/⅓ cup fish stock

140g/5oz tomato sauce

170g/6oz cooked shrimp

1 tsp dried dill

95g/3½oz/1 cup
asiago cheese, grated

¼ tsp calcium

Method

- Preheat oven to 200°C/400°F. Bring a pan of water to a boil, add pasta, and par-boil for about 6 minutes. Drain and set aside.

- Add the garlic, juice from can of tomatoes, and fish stock to the pan. Bring to a boil, reduce heat, and simmer for 5–7 minutes until most of the liquid has evaporated. Stir in the tomatoes and tomato sauce. Bring to a boil. Add the shrimp, pasta, dill, half the cheese, and calcium. Mix thoroughly.

- Transfer to a lightly greased shallow baking dish. Sprinkle the top with the rest of the cheese and bake for 15–20 minutes. Allow to cool to room temperature and serve.

Nutritional info per serving: Calories 1206kcal; Protein 85g;
Carbohydrates 128g; Fiber 22g; Fat 41g; Calcium 1744mg

Rice pilaf

Preparation time: 10 minutes • Cooking time: 30 minutes • Servings: 1

Full of goodness. You can also substitute the beef stock with chicken stock and the beef with chicken, and omit the garlic to make a tummy-friendly meal for your pet.

Ingredients

360g/13oz/2 cups brown rice

475ml/16½fl oz/2 cups
beef stock

2 garlic cloves, crushed

110g/4oz hummus

¼ tsp cinnamon

110g/4oz canned
black beans, mashed

110g/4oz cooked beef, cubed
(or any other meat)

½ tsp calcium

Method

• Bring a pan of water to a boil and par-boil the rice for 10 minutes. Drain.

• Add the stock to the pan, then add the garlic, hummus, cinnamon, black beans, and rice. Stir to mix. Bring back to a boil, reduce heat, and simmer for about 30 minutes, stirring occasionally, until the rice is cooked and the liquid has evaporated. Add more liquid as necessary.

• Allow to cool, stir in the beef and calcium. Place in dog bowl and serve.

Nutritional info per serving: Calories 1046kcal; Protein 66g; Carbohydrates 127g; Fiber 22g; Fat 30g; Calcium 1626mg

Tuna polenta

Preparation time: 10 minutes • Cooking time: 50 minutes • Servings: 2

Fish isn't just for cool cats, it's for hot dogs as well! Add
a vegetable side dish from any of the chapters and you've got
the perfect dinner.

Ingredients

1½ L/2¾ pints/6½ cups water

325g/11oz/2 cups polenta

285g/10oz canned tuna

4 eggs, beaten

50g/1¾oz/½ cup
parmesan, grated

2 tsp cod liver oil

30g/1oz liver, chopped

1¼ tsp calcium

180g/6⅓oz/1 cup cooked
brown rice

110g/4oz tomato paste

Method

- Preheat oven to 180°C/350°F. Bring the water to a boil in a saucepan, add the polenta, reduce the heat, and simmer over medium heat, stirring frequently, for 10–15 minutes until polenta thickens.

- Add the tuna, eggs, parmesan, cod liver oil, liver, and calcium to the polenta. Mix well, then pour into a lightly greased shallow baking dish or pie dish. Bake in the oven for 30–35 minutes.

- While the polenta is cooking, cook the rice according to the instructions. Drain and set aside. When the rice is cool, mix in the tomato paste and divide it into two servings. When the polenta is ready, allow to cool to room temperature. Divide into two servings, cut into bite-sized pieces, and serve with rice.

Nutritional info per serving: Calories 1075kcal; Protein 73g; Carbohydrates 124g; Fiber 12g; Fat 32g; Calcium 2149mg

Lamb with lentils

Preparation time: 10 minutes • Cooking time: 2 hours • Servings: 1

This recipe is based on using lamb shanks, which infuses the whole dish with a wonderful flavor. You can replace the shank with any other cut of lamb or use leftover cooked lamb which will reduce the cooking time.

Ingredients

6 lamb shanks

1 Tbsp corn oil

2 cloves garlic, crushed

2 strips bacon, cut into bite-sized pieces

795g/1lb 2oz/2 cups lentils

100g/3½oz carrots, sliced

55g/2oz celery, cut into bite-sized pieces

475ml/16½oz/2 cups vegetable stock

475ml/16½oz/2 cups water

¾ tsp calcium

Method

- Put the lamb shanks in a large saucepan. In a frying pan heat the oil and sauté the garlic and bacon pieces for 1–2 minutes. Add to the lamb shanks.

- Add the lentils, carrots, and celery. Cover with the vegetable stock and water. Bring to a boil and simmer gently over a very low heat for about 2 hours, adding more liquid as necessary.

- When cooked, remove from heat and allow to cool to room temperature. Remove lamb shanks. Take 85g (3oz) of lamb and place in dog bowl. Pour the rest of the mixture over the lamb. Add calcium and stir to mix well.

Nutritional info per serving: Calories 1071kcal; Protein 64g;
Carbohydrates 92g; Fiber 35g; Fat 51g; Calcium 2330mg

To Share

Magic meal: Take unconditional love, low blood pressure, and no lip, and add our love, our time, and the best food we can. Mix together and you have the recipe for magic moments. Love is... cooking together. Oh ok, so your pups won't be much help, but they will show their appreciation by licking the bowl clean. So, throw a bit extra in the pot and the whole family can eat together.

Avocado and chicken casserole

Preparation time: 20 minutes • Cooking time: 55 minutes

• Servings: 1 dog, 6 human

Dogs just love avocado and it's great for keeping their coats really

glossy. This is a delicious meal which the whole family will find yummy.

Ingredients

340g/12oz/8 cups spinach
noodles or pasta

1 large avocado, peeled and sliced

2 Tbsp fresh lime juice

3 Tbsp olive oil

35g/1¼oz/¼ cup flour

1 tsp cornflour mixed
with a little milk

500ml/19fl oz/2¼ cups
skimmed milk

50g/1¾oz/½ cup cheddar cheese,
grated

3 skinless chicken breasts, diced

Tabasco sauce, optional, for the
human portion

Doggie Version add:
¾ tsp calcium

Method

- Preheat oven to 180°C/350°F. Cook the noodles according to package directions, drain and set aside. Drizzle the avocado slices with lime juice and set aside.

- Heat the oil in a saucepan over low heat. Stir in the flour and cook over low heat until the mixture bubbles. Add the cornflour and milk and mix slowly, stirring constantly until the mixture thickens. Add the cheese and stir until it has melted. Set aside ⅓ of this sauce. Mix the remainder with the cooked noodles.

- Place the chicken in the bottom of a lightly greased baking dish. Spoon the noodle mixture over the chicken. Place avocado slices on top and pour the remaining sauce over the avocados. Bake uncovered for 35 minutes. When cooked, divide mixture in two. In one half, add the calcium, mix well, place in a dog bowl and serve at room temperature. The other half is all yours.

- Add a dash of tabasco sauce to your version to spice up this dish.

Nutritional info per serving: Calories 1405kcal; Protein 85g;
Carbohydrates 153g; Fiber 16g; Fat 53g; Calcium 1755mg

Beef and black bean stew

Preparation time: 5 minutes • Cooking time: 30 minutes

• Servings: 3 dog, 3 human

This is a recipe for your slow cooker or crockpot.

Ingredients

900g/2lb minced beef

2 Tbsp garlic powder

2 x 425-g/15-oz cans
sweet corn, drained

2 x 425-g/15-oz cans
black beans, undrained and mashed

2 x 170-g/6-oz cans tomato paste

700ml/25fl oz/3 cups water

240ml/8½fl oz/1 cup sour cream

450g/1lb/4¾ cups cheddar
cheese, grated

16 pieces corn bread

Doggie Version add:
1 tsp calcium

Method

- Brown the beef in a non-stick frying pan. Mix in the garlic powder. Reduce the heat to low, cover and simmer for 10 minutes.

- In a slow cooker, over low heat, combine the sweet corn, beans, tomato paste, and water. Mix well. Add the beef and sour cream. Raise heat to high setting and simmer for 20 minutes.

- When cooked, divide the mixture into two. For the doggie version add the calcium and mix well. Divide each half of the mixture into 3 servings and sprinkle the cheese over each one. For the doggie version break 2 pieces of corn bread into each serving and serve at room temperature. For humans, serve warm corn bread on the side.

Note: You could also freeze the servings in bags to use another day.

Nutritional info per serving: Calories 1326kcal; Protein 86g; Carbohydrates 116g; Fiber 17g; Fat 58g; Calcium 1325mg

Salmon stroganoff

Preparation time: 10 minutes • Cooking time: 35 minutes

• Servings: 3 dog, 4–6 human

A fishy take on stroganoff. This recipe is a little difficult, but well worth it.

Ingredients

900g/2lb spinach noodles

400g/14oz canned salmon plus
170g/6oz canned mushrooms plus
55g/2oz canned pimentos

350g/12½oz/1½ cups cottage cheese

350g/12½oz/1½ cups sour cream

1 clove garlic, crushed

95g/3½oz/1 cup cheddar cheese

110g/4oz/1 cup breadcrumbs

2 Tbsp corn oil

Dog Version add:

1 tsp calcium

6 Weetabix/100g similar cereal

Human Version add:
120ml/4fl oz/½ cup mayonnaise

3 Tbsp onions, grated

1½ tsp Worcestershire sauce
plus 1 tsp salt

Method

• Preheat oven to 180°C/350°F. In a bowl, combine the noodles, salmon, mushrooms, and pimentos. Combine the cottage cheese, sour cream, and garlic; add to the noodle mixture and mix well. Divide mixture into two portions and in one, stir in the grated cheese and calcium. For the human version, omit the calcium and stir in the mayonnaise, onions, Worcestershire sauce and salt.

• Transfer each version to a greased 2L/4 pint/2qt baking dish. Crush Weetabix (omit for humans) into the breadcrumbs, mix and toss with the oil; sprinkle over each stroganoff. Bake, uncovered, for 30–35 minutes. Serve doggie version at room temperature.

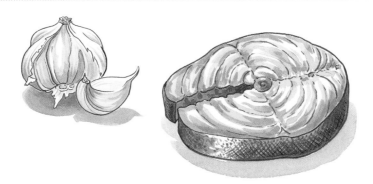

Nutritional info per serving: Calories 1498kcal; Protein 77g; Carbohydrates 145g; Fiber 11g; Fat 67g; Calcium 1924mg

Vegetable rice quiche

Preparation time: 15 minutes • Cooking time: 45 minutes

• Servings: 1 dog, 6 human

This is great for vegetarians. The doggie version has liver to provide

vitamin B12, and there are eggs and cheese for protein.

Ingredients

8 eggs

720g/25oz/4 cups cooked rice

675g/1½lb broccoli, chopped

110g/4oz green peppers, chopped

2 cloves garlic, minced

95g/3½oz/1 cup cheddar cheese, grated

110g/4oz pimento

110g/4oz mushrooms, chopped

240ml/8½fl oz/1 cup skimmed milk

Doggie Version add:
30g/1oz cooked liver, diced

½ tsp calcium

Method

- Pre-heat oven to 190°C/375°F. Beat 2 of the eggs and add to the rice. Stir until well blended. Divide mixture in two. Press half of the mixture onto bottom and up sides of a lightly greased 23cm (9in) plate or shallow baking dish. Repeat to line a second plate or dish with the other half of the mixture. Set aside.

- Add the broccoli, pepper, and garlic to a non-stick frying pan and cook over a medium heat, stirring occasionally until lightly cooked, about 4 minutes. Set aside to cool slightly. Stir in the cheese, pimentos, and mushrooms.

- Divide the mixture in two. For the doggie version, stir in the diced liver and calcium. Spoon each half into the two prepared quiche crusts. In a large bowl, beat together the remaining eggs and milk until well blended. Divide in half and pour over the vegetables in each quiche. Bake until a knife inserted near the center comes out clean, about 35–45 minutes. Let the doggie version cool to room temperature, scoop into dog bowl and serve. The human version can be eaten hot or cold.

Nutritional info per serving: Calories 1211kcal; Protein 72g;
Carbohydrates 133g; Fiber 21g; Fat 46g; Calcium 2294mg

Braised squash with green lentils

Preparation time: 15 minutes • Cooking time: 30 minutes

• Servings: 1 dog, 2 human

A healthy vegetable side dish to go with one of the main meals.

Ingredients

45g/1½oz/½ cup lentils

2 tbs olive oil

2 garlic cloves, crushed

1 sprig fresh thyme, or
1 tsp dried thyme

2 bay leaves

1kg/2¼lb/5 cups butternut squash
or pumpkin, cut into bite-sized pieces

455g/1lb fresh tomatoes, chopped

juice of 1 lemon

Doggie Version add:
⅛ tsp calcium

Method

- Bring a pan of water to a boil and add the lentils. Reduce the heat and simmer over a low–medium heat until soft, about 30 minutes.

- In a large frying pan heat the oil, then sauté the garlic, thyme, and bay leaves for 1–2 minutes. Add the squash, stir together, and cook gently for 6–7 minutes. Drain lentils, add to pan and stir in. Add the tomatoes and cook gently for a further 20 minutes, stirring occasionally. The dish shouldn't be too runny, so allow some of the liquid to evaporate.

- Remove bay leaves and thyme (if using fresh). Divide the mixture in two. In one half stir in the calcium and place in dog bowl with a main course. Allow to cool to room temperature and serve. Enjoy the other half with your own main course.

Nutritional info per serving: Calories 500kcal; Protein 12g; Carbohydrates 93g; Fiber 29g; Fat 15g; Calcium 439mg

Egg and vegetable casserole

Preparation time: 10 minutes • Cooking time: 30 minutes

• Servings: 1 dog, 6 human

This recipe has everything! Eggs (almost the perfect dog food), beans,

vegetables, and whole grains. Good for the whole family.

Ingredients

455g/1lb broccoli	540g/19oz/3 cups cooked barley
225g/8oz red peppers	540g/19oz/3 cups cooked lentils
2 medium sweet potatoes	95g/3½oz/1 cup cheddar cheese, grated
170g/6oz squash	**Doggie Version add:**
12 eggs	1½ tsp calcium
475ml/16½fl oz/2 cups cottage cheese	1½ tsp corn oil
	30g/1oz liver, diced

Method

- Preheat oven to 180°C/350°F. Lightly grease two 23cm (9in) casserole dishes. Peel and dice the vegetables (or use frozen vegetables) and place in a microwave-safe bowl. Cover with plastic wrap and cook on high for 3 minutes. Alternately, boil or steam the vegetables for 3 minutes. Set aside.

- Mix the eggs and cottage cheese in a large bowl. Add the barley and lentils and mix well. Divide the mixture in two. Pour half of this mixture into one of the casserole dishes. Top with half of the well-drained vegetables and grated cheese. Pour half the remaining egg mixture over vegetables. For the doggie version add the diced liver, oil and calcium to the egg mixture and mix well. Pour half this mixture into the other casserole dish, top with the remaining vegetables and cheese, and pour the remaining egg mixture over vegetables.

- Put both casserole dishes in the oven and bake for about 30 minutes. The eggs should be set and the top lightly brown. Cool dog version to room temperature and serve.

Nutritional info per serving: Calories 1252kcal; Protein 85g;
Carbohydrates 134g; Fiber 35g; Fat 45g; Calcium 2041mg

Glazed parsnips and carrots

Preparation time: 10 minutes • Cooking time: 35 minutes

• Servings: 1 dog, 2 human

A yummy vegetable side dish to add to a main course.

Ingredients

310g/11oz parsnips

310g/11oz carrots

2 Tbsp sesame seeds

2 Tbsp olive oil

2 Tbsp maple syrup

zest and juice of ½ orange

Doggie Version add:
⅛ tsp calcium

Method

• Preheat oven to 190°C/375°F. Peel or scrub the parsnips and carrots and cut into bite-sized pieces. Bring a pan of water to a boil, add the carrots and parsnips, and cook for 5 minutes. Drain.

• In a bowl, mix the sesame seeds, olive oil, maple syrup, orange zest, and juice. Pour over the parsnips and carrots. Transfer to a roasting pan and bake in the oven for 15–20 minutes until just brown.

• Divide the vegetables in two. In one half add the calcium and stir to mix. Place in a dog bowl with a main course and serve at room temperature. The rest is for you to enjoy hot, with own your main course.

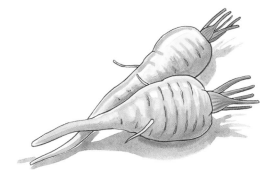

Nutritional info per serving: Calories 396kcal; Protein 5g;
Carbohydrates 54g; Fiber 11g; Fat 20g; Calcium 303mg

Chinese stir-fried vegetables

Preparation time: 15 minutes • Cooking time: 10 minutes

• Servings: 1 dog, 2 human

This quick and easy Asian vegetable dish makes a *pawfect*

accompaniment to a main course.

Ingredients

3 Tbsp sunflower oil

1 tsp sesame oil

2 garlic cloves, crushed

170g/6oz carrots, diced

170g/6oz broccoli, chopped

1 red pepper, de-seeded and chopped

170g/6oz mushrooms, chopped

30g/1oz seaweed (dried seaweed soaked for 10 minutes or dried flakes)

400g/14oz Chinese cabbage, shredded

225g/8oz beansprouts

3 Tbsp soy sauce

Doggie Version add:
⅛ tsp calcium

Method

- Heat oils in large wok. Add garlic and stir-fry for 1–2 minutes. Add the rest of the vegetables and stir-fry until done *al dente* (still a little crisp); about 8 minutes or so. Pour soy sauce over vegetables.

- Divide in two. In one half, add the calcium and stir to mix. Put in dog bowl with main course and serve at room temperature. The rest is all yours!

Nutritional info per serving: Calories 363kcal; Protein 12g; Carbohydrates 33g; Fiber 13g; Fat 24g; Calcium 499mg

Snacks and Treats

Special treats make a welcome change from the boring old dog biscuit. They are the perfect way to fill a rainy afternoon, create the best party, reward your dog, or just enjoy a sunny day. This section includes a delicious cake that your pet and friends (and you, if they allow) can dig in to; yummy ice cream for cooling down on a hot day; fortune telling cookies with a difference; and simply the best way for you both to spend a day in the garden.

Molasses spice cake

Preparation time: 10 minutes • Cooking time: 1 hour • Servings: 15

This is the perfect cake for a chop-lickin' treat.

Ingredients

170g/6oz peanut butter

85g/3oz/⅔ cup brown sugar

3 eggs

240ml/8⅓fl oz/1 cup molasses

240g/10oz/2 cups
whole wheat flour

1 Tbsp lecithin granules

1 tsp ground cinnamon

½ tsp ground ginger

½ tsp ground pumpkin pie spice

240ml/8⅓fl oz/1 cup boiling water

4 tsp baking soda

200g/7oz cream cheese

½ tsp vanilla extract

400g/14oz/2¼ cups icing sugar

1 tsp ground cinnamon

Method

• Preheat oven to 180°C/350°F. Lightly grease a 23cm (9in) cake pan. Beat together the peanut butter and sugar until well mixed. Add the eggs one at a time, beating well after each addition. Add the molasses and blend well.

• In another bowl, combine the flour, lecithin, cinnamon, ginger and pumpkin pie spice, and slowly add to the creamed peanut mixture, beating slowly to blend in.

• Dissolve the baking soda in boiling water (use a big pot as the soda will really froth up). Slowly add to the cake mix, beating slowly to blend in. The mixture will be very runny. Pour into the prepared cake pan and bake in the center of the oven for about 1 hour, or until a toothpick inserted in the center of the cake comes out clean. Leave for about 5 minutes and then set on a wire rack to cool.

• Lightly beat vanilla extract into cream cheese. Sift icing sugar and cinnamon and gradually add to the cream cheese, mixing well. Cover and refrigerate for a few hours to firm up, then use to cover the cake.

Nutritional info per serving: Calories 226kcal; Protein 7g; Carbohydrates 33g; Fiber 3g; Fat 8g; Calcium 214mg

Ice-cream

Preparation time: 5 minutes • Cooking time: 30 minutes • Servings: 10

This recipe is for vanilla ice-cream but you can add any flavor
that you think your doggie will like. Unusual, but yummy for pooches,
is fish. Add 55g (2oz) of cooked, flaked fish to egg mixture before
freezing. Another good flavor is licorice or aniseed. Never use chocolate
because it can be poisonous to dogs, even in small amounts.

Ingredients

2 eggs

475ml/16½fl oz/2 cups light cream

240ml/8⅓fl oz/1 cup milk

2 tsp vanilla extract

¼ tsp calcium

Method

- Beat the eggs until light in color and fluffy; about 1–2 minutes. Beat in the cream and milk. Add the vanilla (and any other flavoring) and calcium and mix well.

- If you have an ice-cream maker, freeze according to the directions. Otherwise put into a freezer-safe container and freeze overnight.

- The more you beat the ice-cream and the more air you incorporate, the softer the ice-cream will be. Sugarless ice-cream tends to be quite hard, so you will need to remove it from the freezer for a few minutes before scooping out a serving.

Nutritional info per serving: Calories 204kcal; Protein 4g; Carbohydrates 3g; Fiber 0g; Fat 20g; Calcium 139mg

Fido fortune cookies

Preparation time: 5 minutes • Cooking time: 5 minutes • Servings: 3

The perfect cookie for a puppy party. Buy or make your own fortunes, place inside the cookies and let your pet and the party guests learn their fate! Nutritional information is based on a serving size of 2 cookies.

Ingredients

1 egg

35g/1¼oz/¼ cup
brown sugar

2 Tbsp sunflower oil

⅛ tsp calcium

30g/1oz/¼ cup cornflour

2 Tbsp water

Method

• Beat the egg and sugar together until thick and smooth. Add the oil and calcium and mix well. Whisk the cornflour into the water and a little of the egg mixture until smooth. Add to the egg mixture and beat well.

• Heat a frying pan to medium heat. Drop a heaped teaspoonful of the batter onto the pan and use a spatula to spread the mixture into a round thin cookie shape about 8cm (3in) in diameter. Brown the cookie on both sides.

• Remove the cookie from pan and, while warm and soft, add fortune paper and fold the cookie in half by pinching the sides together. Place on wire rack to cool and firm up. Use the rest of the mixture up in the same way.

Nutritional info per serving: Calories 191kcal; Protein 2g;
Carbohydrates 22g; Fiber 0.1g; Fat 11g; Calcium 140mg

Cheesy beef bites

Preparation time: 20 minutes • Cooking time: 45 minutes • Servings: 2

The number of cookies you make depends upon how big or small
you cut the dough. The nutritional information is based on
a 55g (2oz) serving. If you have a large dog, you can cut the
dough into bigger cookies.

Ingredients

270g/9½oz/3 cups rolled oats

350ml/10fl oz/1½ cups
lard

710ml/25fl oz/3 cups
boiling water

360g/12¾oz/2¼ cups polenta

3 Tbsp brown sugar

350ml/10fl oz/1½ cups
skimmed milk

280g/10oz/3 cups cheddar
cheese, grated

3 eggs, beaten

1¼kg/2¾lb/9 cups whole
wheat flour

1 Tbsp calcium

Method

• Pre-heat oven to 170°C/325°F. In a large bowl combine the oats, lard, and water. Let stand for 10 minutes. Stir in the polenta, sugar, milk, cheese and eggs. Mix well. Add the flour slowly, with the calcium, kneading well after each addition to form a stiff, smooth dough.

• Break off handfuls of dough and roll into long, round strips about 1cm (½in) wide. Cut into 2.5 cm (1 in) pieces and place on a lightly greased baking tray.

• Bake for about 45 minutes, turning the baking tray around half way through cooking. Turn off the oven and leave to harden for a few hours or overnight. These will keep in an air-tight container for a long time because of their low moisture content.

Nutritional info per serving: Calories 130kcal; Protein 8g; Carbohydrates 20g; Fiber 2.8g; Fat 2.5g; Calcium 184mg

Poochie peanut butter

Preparation time: 0 minutes • Cooking time: 0 minutes • Servings: 1 (2 Tbsp)

This is the best fun you and your pet can have together. Take a summer's

day and sit out in the garden with a jar of peanut butter and your dog.

Ingredients

1 summer's day

1 garden chair

1 much loved dog

1 jar of peanut butter

2 fingers

Method

- Make yourself comfortable in your chair with poochie sitting at your feet. Placing two fingers in the jar of peanut butter, take a generous scoop. Offer to your pet and, if possible, slip peanut butter behind the top front teeth.

- Sit back and watch his/her tongue work overtime.

Nutritional info per serving: Calories 188kcal; Protein 8g; Carbohydrates 7g; Fiber 3g; Fat 16g; Calcium 14mg

Index